# PATHWAYS

# TO ACADEMIC

# SUCCESS

JOE-JESIMIEL OGBE

JOE JESIMIEL OGBE

Pathways to Academic Success

Copyright- 2018 Joe Jesimiel Ogbe

ISBN - 978-978- 55429-3-6

Published in Nigeria by:

Young Disciples Press

For Further information or permission, contact:

Director of Publication

Young Disciples International (YDI)

3, YDI Street,

Off Isheri-Lasu Express Road

By Soulos Hotel Bus-Stop,

Igando, Lagos, Nigeria.

Tel. 08023124455, 08033475807, 01-2934286

# CONTENTS

TALENT IS NEVER ENOUGH

# DEDICATION

To Dr. Adeyemi Adeleye, popularly called the Academic god in YDI family, for his outstanding academic excellence over the years!

# FORWORD

In the book "Pathways to Academic Success" the author, Joe Jesimiel Ogbe, explicitly captures practical conceptions of academic success and failure. The book, in its entrancing introduction and seven (7) chapters, brings clearly into perspective, the spirituality element, a vital ingredient missing in many books on academic success, which is, the God-factor. The book is illuminating as well as instructive in the useful nuggets expounded for driving excellent study habits while avoiding the snares of failure.

The anecdotes from diverse but familiar situational accounts presented, provide clarity for the reader in relating to the subject of the discourse presented. The writing style is simple, conversational and compelling. It is a must read for students at all levels who want to make a headway in their quest to attain excellence and scale greater heights in their academic journey, while serving as an indisputable directional compass to expressly navigate the pathways leading to academic success.

**Prof Aize Obayan,**

Former VC, Covenant University, Ota.

# ENDORSEMENTS

Do you deserve knowledge, then seek for it!

Do you want to succeed in your academic pursuits? Then, "Pathways to Academic Success" a book written by Joe Jesimiel Ogbe is the guide you need.

The author in his latest book brought his over thirty years rich experience of working with the youth to bear on this manual - broaching such sensitive issues as why some students fail, knowing how to read effectively which must have been gathered from the kindergarten centre run by the wife, etc etc and the all important question of the God factor in order to succeed in your academic pursuits.

The seven chapters booklet is a must read for students, teachers and the general public and it is highly recommended as a student's companion.

**Senator Bode Olajumoke, PhD.**

Chancellor, Achievers University, Owoh,
Former Pro-Chancellor, Adekunle Ajasin University,
Akungba

---

This small, short, simple, sound, sweet and well-written smart book is loaded with the necessary ingredients required to add value, in any person's journey, who wants to achieve academic excellence. It is a masterpiece I have come across in recent years. I strongly endorse it without any hesitation.

**Prof. Bala Dogo,**

Former Dean,
Postgraduate School, Kaduna State University

---

I am enthralled to write an endorsement for this timely book, "Pathways to Academic Success" which provides powerful answers to the very many issues which students face in their academic pursuits with each chapter serving as tablet or injection to cure the "deadly disease" of academic failure. May I commend the author for the inspiration, motivation, zeal and determination to come up with this masterpiece at this time.

I hereby endorse this book and recommend that every school library must have copies on their shelves to assist their students in achieving academic success. For every student who wants to say goodbye to academic failure, this book should become your reading and reference companion.

**Mrs. Faith Fatuyi**

Proprietress, Breakthrough Academy, Akute.

This is it! Reading through the book, "Pathways to Academic Success" by Joe Jesmiel Ogbe reminded me of the principles I engaged in as a student from my secondary school through to the University in my undergraduate and postgraduate studies.

Do you really desire sustainable academic success across all levels of schooling? Then, let the author show you the way in this rich and concise book. Here is a tool to change the tides! No more academic failure and stagnation!

You have the pathways in this concise compendium of knowledge.
Go for it!
**Abraham Owoseni**

First Class Graduate of Architecture
Chartered Architect, Educator, Career & Life Coach
Founder & Team Lead, Young Breeds

If you are passionate about Academic Success, this book is the key to unlock it. Having been a beneficiary of the teachings of the Author, Joe Jesimiel Ogbe, in my own sojourn to become a qualified Chartered Accountant, I have no doubt that putting what we have learnt from him over the years into writing in this book will not only propel multitude to success but will lead to the emergence of academic stars.

The book does not only address the foundations required for good success, it provides time-tested principles required to stand out in life. Studying this book will not only boost the morale and interest of students with declining performance, it will also enhance the success of those who are already doing well and desire to do better and maximise their God-given abilities.

I'm recommending this book to all my students and all who have the desire to succeed in their academics.

**Lekan Salami Bsc,** MBA, ACTI, FCA
- CEO Rays of Hope Int'l School
- Managing Partner Lekan Salami & Co. (Chartered Accountants)
- MD/CEO DBC Professionals Ltd

---

"...I learnt early in my quest for success that preparation is the secret of success...the best way to prepare for academic success is to be armed with requisite knowledge; this knowledge is what Joe Jesimiel Ogbe has packaged in this great book...Read it, apply its principles and academic excellence is assured..."

**Dr. Azubuike Ezenwoke,**
Registrar, Landmark University & Founder, the "A" Student Summit

---

This is the academic Solution masterpiece!

In your hand is not only a frank acknowledgement of the current disturbing academic problem among our youths today but most importantly a giant step taken in proffering solutions to the challenge of academic failure which has bedevilled many youths.

Mass failures in WAEC, SSCE, NECO, and GCE in recent years have reached alarming rate in the country that the various government agencies are now crying out on the urgent need to stop the ugly trend. Our universities are not spared in this sad situation.

Joe Jesimiel Ogbe, in this easy-to-read book, has brought to bear his wealth of ministerial experience in youth and students ministry to address the ugly challenge head-long. He has provided a tool capable of reversing the declining rate of education in Nigeria.

Having personally read through this great work, I am convinced that students, counsellors and teachers will find this work very helpful.

**Rev. Emeka Ngubo**
Chairman/CEO, Elim Motors Ltd, Lekki Lagos

It gives me a great pleasure to endorse this addition to the literary world from the stable of the author, Joe Jesimiel Ogbe. Thomas Edison, the man regarded as America's greatest inventor and discoverer of the electric light bulb, said that "Genius is one percent inspiration and ninety-nine percent perspiration." There is no lasting success without both elements – inspiration and perspiration. I believe that Pastor Joe has provided these dual tools through his book, "Pathways to Academic Success". It will provide a needed booster to the discovery of your purpose, and keeping a steady eye on your goal as you pursue your education. The book is well laid out and easy to comprehend. Aspiring and life-long students will find it to be a good self-motivation resource. I wholeheartedly recommend it to parents who desire to encourage their children to excel in their academics; and to students who want a material that will always keep up their momentum as they study and push them to the limit of their academic success.

**Pastor Oladipo Ajayi,**

President, Dominion Cares, Minnesota USA and Gloria Charities International, (An Education-Focused Non-Profit Organization.)

---

Looking at the contents and my personal life story in retrospect, I am aware of some major reasons why students fail examinations. Since I was not a Christian at the time of my secondary education until my university days, I didn't know anything about vision or discovering God's plan for one's life. I was not also aware that as a student you have to major in your primary purpose/objective and pay most attention diligently to reading and studying as a student if you actually intend to succeed academically. This book brought to the forefront the effective reading habits as a major criterion and strategy for provoking unending academic success in life.

The God-factor in all academic endeavours in life cannot be overemphasized. Unknown to many people who thought I was an A grade student all through my academic journey, that was not true. I had one primary school classmate by name Ojo Shaibu who later became Dr. Onukaba Adinoyi Ojo. (PhD). We did primary six and seven together in the then Kwara State between 1971 and 1972 respectively. We attended St. Matthew primary school Ogboroke, Ihima and he topped the national common entrance examination result with 88% while I came second with 85% in 1972. We both got admission into Igbirra Anglican College now Lennon Memorial College, Ageva- Okene in January 1973 on merit.

At graduation in June 1977, while my colleague led the chart again, with Aggregate 15 and came out in Division one, among the 42 students who passed the WASC examination out of 68 students who sat for the examination: 7 students earned grade one, 8 students came out in grade two and another set of 27 students got grade three. I had Aggregate 45 with statement of result (SR) so I was not among the 42 students who made it then. With SR, I didn't pass and neither did I fail, I was hanging in a balance. I had failed to my greatest surprise so I sat down one day in 1978, this time in Martins College Issele-uku where I had gone to obtain a Teachers grade two certificate since I was unable to make the WAEC. I got thinking and you know failure gives you both pain and regret in life. I challenged myself in 1978 to succeed academically at all costs and I made my late primary school classmate my role model for my intended success. That was one of my strategy and pathway to success.

By God's grace today, in that class of 68 students, who sat for the 1977 WASC, if the class is re-arranged now, I am back to my second position of 1972 then in primary seven. That is what is called breakthrough academically if you like. Someone may ask why? Because today, I am privileged to be one of the only three (3) Doctorial degrees graduates that have been produced by the 1977 set till date, having earned a PhD in Entrepreneurship Development Studies. I must admit here that certainly the major factor to my academic success in life is nothing but the GOD factor which unfortunately youths don't take seriously most of the time at that age.

This book is a must-have and read for all categories of students in all levels of educational strata and ipso-factor I recommend it for all educational institutions as an essential study material for examination success purpose.

**Pastor Michael Makeyoh OLADUN** (PhD, MNIM)
Managing Director/CEO,
Crystal Expertise Resources Ltd & Crystal Academy Schools,
Lagos, Nigeria.

# INTRODUCTION

In my over 32 years working with young people as a youth and students' minister, I have come to realise that academic failure is one of the grave challenges bedevilling and traumatising many of them, hence my resolve to write this book. Having prayed for and counselled many of them, I know where the shoe pinches! I know what it takes for the so-called dullard to become an academic success in a jiffy. This book is my modest attempt to motivate, spur and help every struggling student to work their way to outstanding success.

The fact of life is that success has many friends while failure has none. Failure is like a poor man who is hated even by his own neighbour, while success is akin to a rich man with many friends.

In the course of writing, the Super Eagles of Nigeria were on fire in their Group D match against Iceland with Ahmed Musa scoring two goals in the second half to beat Iceland 2-0 and move from bottom to second place in Volgograd on Friday, 22nd June at Russia 2018 World Cup. Social media has been awash with exciting comments from fans who were not pleased with the defeat the Super Eagles suffered in their opening match against Croatia. Nigeria was mercilessly trashed, with a goal margin of 2 -0!

After their woeful defeat, many people turned against them, calling them unpleasant and unprintable names. Failure or defeat in life is not the best as nobody would like to identify with failure. In many years that I have worked with young people, I am yet to see any youth giving testimonies of failures!

Have you ever felt like giving up on your academic dreams? Many students felt more. You are not the only one! There were times when they completely felt like throwing in the towel. A time when they thought they weren't worthy to live up to their dreams of becoming stars on the academic corridor.

As a student, do you have the lethargy to read or a disdain for serious academic work?

Do you want to experience a change from abysmal failure to sterling success in your academic work?

Do you want your class or course mates, family, friends and even your entire campus to celebrate you?

Then be prepared and willing to accept and embrace the success- provoking pathways and strategies I will be sharing with you in this portable but powerful book. I am personally persuaded that you will become an academic wonder, if you decide deliberately and concertedly to change your academic story.

Yes, you can re-write your academic story!

Yes, you can alter your past academic failure!

Yes, you can improve on your current academic results!

As a student, have you attained all the academic goals you have set for yourself? If not, don't worry as I will avail you the strategies to achieving your goals. No student wants to remember their failures. It's a negative emotion to feel you have failed. But if you recognise the reasons behind each failure, you will be able to avoid making the same mistakes again. In this book, you will get to understand why students fail academically. For instance, many fail just because they do not really know the purpose or reason why they are in school or pursuing a particular course of study. The truth is that the discovery of academic purpose is fundamental to your quest to obtaining academic excellence. I will help you to develop a sense of purpose!

No excellent student attained success by chance, but by choice! I quite agree with Abigail Adams who said, "Learning is not attained by chance, it must be sought for with ardor and diligence." This book will spur you to become a diligent student. As a student, you must diligently know how to read and study effectively, as reading and studying is crucial and fundamental to your academic success. Reading and studying is one of the most important drivers of any academic endeavour. I will be teaching you how to read and study effectively, via the reading strategy of **SQ3R!**
**(Survey, Question, Read, Recall and Review)**
This is a useful technique that will help you read purposefully and with outstanding results.

Most importantly, I shall be unveiling the main factor that procures excellence not just in your academic work but in life generally. I call it the G-Factor! It is the God factor in your academic pursuit. It is the influence, and power of God helping you in your academic work. Jesus Christ says, "... for without me ye can do nothing." And this includes your academic work. You cannot excel except God is on your side.

Beloved student, I don't care for how long you have been struggling academically. I don't care the number of failures you have suffered in the past. What I care about is that you have the power to alter your academic destiny if you are determined to succeed.

Come on board with me as I show you how to take responsibility for your academic success!

**Joe Jesimiel Ogbe**
October, 2018.

# CHAPTER
## *1*
## Understanding Why Some Students Fail

There are a plethora of reasons some students are experiencing failures in their academic pursuits. Let's consider a few in this opening chapter.

### 1. Voluntary and Involuntary Reason

Some students are failing simply because of involuntary and voluntary reasons. Voluntarily, some fail because they have made up their minds not to engage in any serious academic work. They approach their studies with levity, laziness and nonchalance. It's like they are simply satisfied with poor grades. What a pity! I remember counseling one student who was the "goal keeper" of his class. I mean the one who usually takes the last position in class. My experience with him showed me clearly that there are some students who will never do well academically because they have made up their minds for failure. This student told me in clear terms that he was not designed for academics. With all my persuasive prowess, I tried to motivate him to see why pursuit of academic success is wise and a worthy choice. I regret to say that I was unable to help out. Truly, life is a choice! You are what you are today by the choices you've made in your life journeys. Students who have rigidly made choices not to work hard in their academic pursuit cannot be helped. To such students, I advise that they choose other pursuits, such as skill acquisition in arts and crafts, carpentry, plumbing, fashion designing, tailoring and what have you!

But there are students whose cases are involuntary. They are failing without knowing why they are failing. They love to read and even be in class but they don't have a conscious or deliberate control of their will on how to excel academically. To such students, they can be helped as they could be motivated and encouraged. No amount of motivation or encouragement will hold sway if a student is not just interested in academic work!

## 2.      Sickness or illness: a veritable reason

This is another veritable reason why some students fail in their academic pursuit. I see sickness as a robber of one's academic destiny. A student who is plagued or bedeviled by one sickness or the other cannot think or dream of academic success. Excelling in academics can never be a consideration if the sickness troubling a student is chronic. I know some students who were always rushed home for medical attention even during examinations. No doubt, sickness was the major reason why they did not do well in their exams.

There was this boy in our class when I was in secondary school that we nicknamed sleepyhead, because he would virtually sleep in class all through the day. It was later that we found out that he was plagued with sleeping sickness, called human African trypanosomiasis, which is a widespread tropical disease that can be fatal if not treated. It is spread by the bite of an infected tsetse fly (Glossina Genus), a specie native to the African continent.

To achieve your academic goals you must proactively take care of your physical and mental health. Aim to eat healthily and keep to an ideal weight, drink plenty of water, avoid smoking and exercise daily. Even if it's just a short walk, there is so much you can derive from bodily exercises. Exercise releases endorphins, which increase your levels of happiness, help you work harder and achieve more academically. That's why we have time for games and sports in school.

### 3.    Wrong Company

Do you want academic success to accompany you? Then keep company with success-driven students! Do you want failure to be your second name? Then company or move with students that are on the highway to failure by choice!

Bishop David Oyedepo said, "The company you keep determines what accompanies you!"

No doubt, wrong company will rob any student of success! Some students fail in their academic pursuit simply because they are foolish to keep company with students who do not take their academic work seriously. Show me your friend, and I will predict accurately and veritably what lies ahead of you academically.

Don't keep company with any student that abandons or stabs classes!
Don't keep company with any group of students that don't take their academic work seriously!
Do keep company with students that have superior inclination and drive for academic success!

## 4.     Inferiority Complex

Some students fail academically due to inferiority complex. A student that I counseled, not too long ago, suffered the plague of academic failure, having been molested by inferiority complex. This student was put down by her parents, teachers and classmates who never saw anything good in her. She eventually joined discouragers to put herself down. Her mother in particular was always complaining and comparing her with her siblings right from when she was a kid. She saw herself from the eyes or views of her mother and began to evaluate herself as inferior. Her inferiority complex affected her academic results negatively, as she failed abysmally.

My candid advice is that you should not allow anybody to compare you with another human being! You are you! Nobody can be like you. You can never be a clone of your brother, sister or friend! You are a special person created uniquely by God. It's not good to compare yourself with anybody. You are not wise if you do so!

In God's sight no man or woman is inferior! Place value on yourself. Don't get into self pity! Self-pity is a form of self affliction whereby you permit yourself to indulge in thoughts of incapability until you become thoroughly miserable. And when you become miserable, you lack the momentum or agility to read your books. A student who sees no prospect of being successful academically is like a man trapped in Sahara desert with nothing but kilometres of hot sand in all direction. His tongue becomes swollen with thirst, he falls on the desert floor awaiting death. He is utterly hopeless! Without hope, there is no joy. Without joy, there is no desire to read or study.

## 5.    Lack of Money

Lack of money is another major reason why some brilliant students have jettisoned the idea or hope of furthering their education! As we all know that money is the fuel of any given project! Money answers all things, and this includes worthy academic pursuit. In many parts of the world, students are becoming extremely scared of pursuing academic dreams due to education costs. Don't allow lack of money to frustrate your academic pursuits.

Help could come your way even from quarters you least expect. An uncle or aunt of yours could help if you are that brilliant and interested in education. I have volunteered to help some indigent students who cannot afford the cost of education. There are some organizations that are offering scholarships to students. You can take advantage of such opportunities. Two of my protégés are schooling abroad today not because their parents could afford it, but because I advised them to try academic scholarships or grants online. Both of them were fortunate to secure scholarships to pursue their dream courses at their dream universities. One outstanding factor for their scholarships was that both of them had first class degrees. One of them, Tunde Alawode by name, was the best graduating student from university of Lagos. You can't take your academic work seriously and not find a sponsor somewhere to help out!

## 6.    Parental Interference

It will surprise you to know that some parents are even the major reason their children are not doing well academically. I have counseled some parents who have been interfering and frustrating their children's academic pursuits just because they feel their children should read a particular course. What about a father who even vowed that over his death will his son read another course. As a lawyer, he wanted his son to read law so that his son could take over his chambers when he dies. What this father failed to realize was that his son was not cut out for law at all, as he was not good in the arts but extremely good in the sciences. Forcing him to read law is like forcing a fish to climb trees like a monkey. I have advised parents over and over to stop insisting that their daughter or son must study a particular course. Students should be allowed to read the courses that they are cut out for or good at.

## 7.     Fear of failure and low Self-esteem

Fear has torment! There is nothing that torments a student like fear of failure. But what causes the fear of failure? Lack of adequate preparation!

You will be scared stiff or fearful if you fail to prepare well enough. To pass an exam you need to prepare adequately for it. Students who fail to prepare until few days or weeks, or wait until the last minute will surely be afraid of exams.

The Bible says, "And he said, I am God, the God of thy father: fear not to go down into Egypt; for I will there make of thee a great nation:" (Genesis 46:3)

In our context, God is saying you should not be afraid to go for that test or exams as He will be there for you. But make sure you have read and studied well enough.

Low self-esteem is like fear of failure. It can also work against your success. Low self-esteem or lack of self-confidence can prevent you from building on your strengths or confront any academic challenge. Have a healthy self-esteem! Don't be overconfident, as overconfidence can be counterproductive. Only students with healthy self-confidence that can command outstanding results. Overconfidence can prevent you from acknowledging and improving on your weaknesses. Some overconfident students don't even believe they have any weakness at all, as such they don't usually ask for help from their teachers or classmates.

I'm not promoting over dependence on others to succeed. No! Rather I'm advocating that students develop healthy self-esteem, robust academic independence and accountability so that from the moment they enter school they will have more prospect to succeeding than those that are given to fear and low self-esteem.

Whatever reason is hindering you right now in the pursuit of your academic success can be destroyed or shattered if you engage wisdom, by asking for help from right materials, individuals or quarters.

# CHAPTER
## *2*
## Purpose Discovery: A Major Pathway

D o you really know why you are in school? Do you really know the purpose or reason why you are pursuing a particular course of study?

The discovery of academic purpose is fundamental to your quest to obtaining academic success. There are so many students today who are just drifting about campus without the faintest idea of academic purpose. Many don't know why they are in school, no wonder they are struggling and stranded in their academic pursuit. It is very pathetic to see a great number of students not taking their academic assignments seriously, and this is because many of them do not know why they are in school.

A wise man said, "If a purpose of a thing is not known abuse is inevitable." The primary purpose for being in school is for you to thrive in your academic work. You've got academic work to do!

A student who has discovered the purpose for being in school will never abuse the privilege of being sent to school. Passing out of school or university without a tangible result of academic excellence is a validation that you have abused purpose. When you do not know your Academic Purpose you will join the company of NFAs. I mean, No Future Ambition!

Don't abuse academic purpose by engaging in frivolities! Don't abuse academic purpose by engaging in things that do not add value to your academic results! Don't spend time playing around school or campus as if you're in school for social contest!

If you understand the reason why your parents or guardians are paying so much for your education, you will work assiduously in order to achieve academic excellence. Living out the purpose you were sent to school will spur you to command above average in your exams.

Knowing your academic purpose will make you focus more on your academic life. It will increase your motivation and prepare you for uncommon academic success.

God is a God of purpose! He did not create the earth in vain. He created it to be inhabited and today the earth is fulfilling purpose. "For thus saith the LORD that created the heavens; God himself that formed the earth and made it; he hath established it, he created it not in vain, he formed it to be inhabited: I am the LORD; and there is none else" (Is 45:18).

The discovery of your academic purpose as a student is the beginning of your success story.

A student who is purpose-driven has more value to add to his or her academic life than the other person who is not driven by purpose.

Do you have an idea of academic success and what it means to receive academic awards?
Are you willing to sacrifice your comfort in order to succeed academically?
Great academicians are not born! They are made! They have a clear reason they are burning the midnight candle to excel academically.

**Developing a sense of purpose**

The easiest way to develop a sense of purpose in your academic endeavour is to place a value on your course, and determine exactly the long-term results and rewards that await you.

To develop a sense of purpose, dare to:

1.      Imagine or envision the kind of person you'd like to become, when you're done with school.
2.      Imagine or picture in your mind how your academic pursuits fit into the bigger picture in the future.
3.      Imagine or envision how your family and friends will celebrate you on your graduation day.

4.      Imagine or picture in your mind how your success story will impact other students positively.

5.      Imagine or dream how you will be empowered to contribute to the good of others.

# CHAPTER
## *3*
## The Pathway Of Diligence

Purpose-driven students are extremely diligent. You can only be diligent in your work if you see or perceive profit in it. The virtuous and diligent woman in the book of Proverbs saw profit and got motivated to labour sacrificially in the night.

"She perceiveth that her merchandise is good: her candle goeth not out by night." (Pro 31:18)

Purpose-driven students usually see or perceive profit in their academic work, hence their lamp does not go out at night, as they vigorously engage in reading and studying for tests and exams.

Purpose-driven students know that they can have nothing worthwhile but what they strive for. They know why they are stretching and stretching academically. No excellent student attained success by chance! No! I quite agree with

Abigail Adams who said, "Learning is not attained by chance, it must be sought for with ardor and diligence."

Becoming a diligent student is about your determination not to wait for good luck to succeed in your academic work or pursuit. Rather, it is your decision and your resolve to constantly, earnestly and persistently exert your body and mind to achieve sterling results. Benjamin Franklin said, "Diligence is the mother of good luck."

As a student, when you give your academic work all it takes, nothing or nobody can stop you from standing out academically. Diligence is about giving your best efforts to your academic assignments. It is your resolve to keep reading and studying longer than anyone else.

Great rewards await the diligent student!
You will always be rewarded in direct proportion to the value of your academic contribution.
If you want to increase the size of your rewards, you must increase the quality and quantity of your contribution or results.
Do you want to be rich academically?
Then refuse to be lazy! The Bible says, "He becometh poor that dealeth with a slack hand: but the hand of the diligent maketh rich."
Proverbs 10:4

Diligent students become rulers and dominate the lazy ones. I'm yet to see an average student becoming a head boy or head girl. I'm yet to see a failure representing the school in any academic competition. "The hand of the

diligent shall bear rule: but the slothful shall be under tribute."
Proverbs 12:24

Only the diligent and successful students do stand before VIPs. I mean very important personalities in the society. So if you want to meet and interact with great and successful people, then you must become a diligent student. "Seest thou a man diligent in his business? he shall stand before kings; he shall not stand before mean men." Proverbs 22:29

It takes diligence to know the state of your academic work. It takes diligence to know the number of books or assignments you were given by your teachers or lecturers. Diligence is persisting in your work until you succeed. Someone said, "Great works are performed not by strength, but by perseverance." Every great assignment will require persistence to command great results. Your ability to decide what you want, to begin and then to persist through all obstacles and difficulties until you achieve your goals is the critical determinant of your success.

A diligent student is never afraid of exams or tests! He has developed the courage and boldness to confront any test or exam that may be given. Every fear of exams will evaporate if you have read and studied well ahead. The truth is that fear and ignorance go together. Fear can be caused by ignorance. When you have limited information, you may be tense and insecure about the outcome of your exams. The very act of gathering more information in a particular subject gives you more courage and confidence in that subject. As a driver, I don't have fear of driving. You know why? Because I have mastered the act of driving. As a diligent student, you don't need to fear writing any test or exams, because you must have become dexterous in reading and studying.

The future belongs to the diligent, not to the lazy student! Be prepared to go the extra mile in your academic work. David was asked to bring 100 foreskins of the philistines and he brought 200 instead. That's a diligent young man to emulate!

Thomas Jefferson said, "The rising sun has never caught me in bed in my entire life." Resolve today to at least get up one hour earlier and get going immediately. Diligence is about rising up early and putting action to what you have planned. Plan your days and hours very carefully. Be a good time manger.

Try to give account of your day! Don't waste your time or day!

Do you want to stay ahead of others in your class or course? Then embrace diligence as a lifestyle.

# CHAPTER
## *4*
## Interest: A Major Key To Academic Success

No doubt, interest is a major key to academic success! Students that lack interest in their academic work cannot amount to anything worthwhile. Interest is about you having the feeling of excitement in wanting to read and study your books. It is about you enjoying reading and studying. It is also about you being delighted in academic tests and exams.

Do you love or enjoy reading for long hours without being tired? Do you love the company of bookworms? Are you usually excited when you're asked to come for tutorials or go to the library to read? Are you enthusiastic or happy attending classes?

If "NO!" to any of the questions above, then you may have to do extra work on yourself to boost interest.

Do you realise that it is when you are interested in your studies that you will be able to pursue academic success? So by all means, try to motivate yourself to enjoy reading books. Be a bookworm! Without interest, you will be unenthusiastic about engaging in your academic work.

**Embrace Self-motivation**

Self-motivation is your disposition or ability to motivate or encourage yourself to read or study in the face of lack of interest. Don't forget it is interest that will help you to assimilate whatever you're reading. You can read the best books and other academic materials in the world, but if you're not interested, you will not be able to assimilate any piece of information or assemble facts.

Are there magical formulas to boost interest in academic work? Not really! And this is because individuals have different and unique factors which affect their interest in academic work. Many students study for different reasons and as such they are motivated differently.

In chapter two, I tried to eminently address the issue of purpose. Students who understand why they are in school in the first place will never find it difficult to be self-motivated. They naturally become interested and enthusiastic about learning, working hard, and pushing themselves to excel.

Try to be happy and enthusiastic about your subject. This is very important as not all teachers are happy teaching these days. Many are into teaching profession as a stop-gap measure. So don't look for a teacher's enthusiasm before getting self motivated. Enthusiasm, happiness and passion are contagious. Try to keep company with your classmates who have positive energy or attitude toward their academic work. They are very likely going to influence you positively. Get excited about reading with them.

## High Expectation

Do you know that your parents and siblings have high but attainable expectations of you?

My younger brother passed his difficult medical school exams because of my high expectation which had a powerful effect on his performance. He knew that I was going to reward him handsomely. By my expectation-pressure, I was able to help him set achievable academic goals for himself. He was labouring extra-time to pass. And he passed! Interest will make you to be actively involved in any learning process. You will find it fun trying to solve problems and work on projects with other students. Believe me, social interaction can get you excited about things in the classroom even as other students can motivate you to read and study effectively.

Without a doubt, expectation of rewards, accolades and honours are key aspects of boosting your interest. Interested students are more receptive, learn better, and, as a result, learn more. If you want to learn, then consciously develop interest.

Don't wish that you have interest in your academic work like others, rather work assiduously to be interested. Our people say, life doesn't give you what you wish, but what you work for.

## Boost interest by watching videos of successful people

If you really want to boost interest in your academic work, you can do so by watching videos of successful people, especially students that are doing very well in their academic work. There are many interest-boosting videos that can add value to you. The other day I was watching a video online where Bill Gates was talking about some books he had read and I felt interested in reading those books too. What brought about the interest? I got my interest boosted because a successful person had read such a book!

As a person, apart from being an avid reader, these days I love watching videos of successful people for inspiration on YouTube. I learn a lot from those that have gone ahead of me in life, especially from people in my field. You too can do the same thing, try to watch educational videos quite often, and see how much your interest will be boosted!

## Embrace Perseverance

Success in any area of human endeavour will require perseverance. Interest-boosting in your academic work needs commitment and persistence. You need to demonstrate perseverance, not giving up no matter what!

The truth is that many failure-plagued students easily give up on the verge of success or breakthrough. If you have interest in your studies, giving up will not be an option. You will hang in there, trying to make a difference.

Imagine just for a minute if all excellent students or first class materials that we celebrate today lacked perseverance, they wouldn't be celebrated with awards and gifts.

My sincere prayer is that you may possess an insatiable interest or desire in your academic work so that you may become a template of academic success in your school. Say, Amen!

# CHAPTER

## 5

## Knowing How To Read Effectively

Your ability to read and write is crucial and fundamental to your academic excellence. Reading and studying is one of the most important drivers of any academic endeavour.

Do you know how to read and study?

Do you know why you must read in the first place?

In this chapter I shall be showing you how to engage in effective reading. If you get it right in your reading endeavour, you will get it right in your academic endeavour.

**Before reading, dream success!**

Do you have a dream of becoming an academic champion? You are a success ready to happen if you can picture yourself receiving academic rewards or awards. Dreams will make you ready and prepared to read and study with a view to achieving your academic goals. Students that read usually dream or visualise themselves succeeding in every test or exam they write.

**Before reading, think Success!**

If success is not in view, reading will be out of view!

Top students are always mentally ready before reading or studying. Before you start reading, try to control your mind for success. If you succeed at the mind realm, you will succeed in your reading. Battle for effective reading begins in your mind. Let your thinking be about how you will attain success via reading. Good thinking, good product! Success thinking equals success in reading! And success in reading equals academic success!

Every success starts in the mind. Proverbs 4:23 says, "Be careful what you think, because your thoughts run your life" (NCV). The battle for academic excellence is won or lost in your mind. Any time you see students really messing up in their academic work, you can bet their problems didn't start with their actions, because their actions began with their thoughts. They lingered on dumb thoughts before making dumb decisions.

Don't forget, poor or negative thinking will never procure academic excellence!

**Before reading, develop reason for reading!**

Top students engage in reading purposefully! They know why they are reading. They know what they are looking for. Until you have a strong personal reason for excellence, you may not love reading or studying, as the ability to succeed usually requires a strong personal reason for wanting to succeed. A wiseman said, "Whenever there is a strong personal reason to win or succeed, one finds great amount of unused resources to use."

**Before reading, try to speak to yourself!**

Before settling down to read try to engage in positive affirmations with a view to generating strong belief, and this belief can procure action for effective reading. Offer yourself emotional support by speaking to yourself. For instance, you can say:

"I can do all things through Christ who strengthens me! I can read with understanding through Christ Jesus. I can read for hours without getting tired. I am the finest reader in this class. I'm the best reader. No one can beat me when it comes to reading..."

Do you remember Mohammed Ali, the boxing world champion of all time? He was well known for how he shouted his affirmations before entering the boxing ring. His most well known affirmations were: "Float like a butterfly, sting like a bee. Nobody can beat Mohammad Ali." and "I am the greatest of all time." People thought he was arrogant because of the way he was shouting these affirmations. Later he revealed that he repeated them only for himself because he was so afraid of entering the boxing ring. By repeating those affirmations he developed the winning mindset.

Apart from speaking to yourself before reading, you can also speak or declare success to yourself before starting your exams! It pays to prepare yourself emotionally via positive affirmation.

## Practical Tips for Effective Reading

Goals or blueprints are the greatest source of energy. You can navigate effectively if you have the map or blueprints of where you are going. To command effectiveness you have to practically draw out your blueprint of when, what, where, who and how to read:

1. Decide and know exactly when you want to read. Ask yourself: "Is it in the morning, afternoon or at night?"
2. Decide and know exactly what books, chapters or topics you want to read.
3. Decide and know exactly where you want to read! Ask yourself: "Is it my room, classroom or library?"
4. Decide and know exactly who you want to read with! Ask yourself: "Am I reading alone, with friends or course mates?"
5. Decide and know exactly the number of hours you want to put in! Ask yourself: "Am I reading for one, two, three or five hours?"

## Two Types of Reading

1.      Reading for Academic Study

2.      Reading for Leisure

Reading for academic study is quite different from reading for leisure. For instance, when you're reading for academic study you would be more serious and focused than when you are reading for leisure. The way you read a novel will be quite different from the way you read your text books!

I read novels for pleasure! I read novels from cover to cover but in the case of academic reading, I try to be more selective. I deliberately and concertedly pick chapters or pages that are relevant to the subject I'm researching. I read effectively when I question and survey the text to gain a better understanding of my subject.

The essence of this book is to help you succeed academically, hence my candid advice is that you must read to gain and understand information, and develop ideas. Be selective about what you read, and remember you can't read everything. Don't spend time reading in details without first checking how relevant the text is. As you read, make sure you jot down notes to help you remember vital points. Your notes will prove useful when writing assignments and revising for exams.

As you read or study, take regular breaks. Reading for about 30 or 40 minutes should be enough to really focus on the text and take in as much as possible. Make reading fun by taking a break. Have a recess to take walk around and chat with other students. Try to read in a positive environment that is comfortable and free of distractions as this will help improve your concentration and assimilation.

### Use An Effective Reading Strategy - SQ3R

(Survey, Question, Read, Recall and Review).

This is a useful technique that will help you read purposefully and with outstanding results.

**Survey -** It is about looking over your reading material critically. It is also about skimming through the text to get a general idea of what it is about and help you to decide whether it is of any use to you.

**Question-** Question in this context is about you asking whether or not the text will be of help to you. For instance, ask whether this text contains useful information that you can use. Asking questions will help you to stay focused on your subject.

**Reading -** You must consciously make effort at careful and detailed reading of the text. Be focused and mentally follow salient points in the course of reading the text. Make notes of any key points.

**Recall -** Do you usually remember what you have read or learned? Until you can bring a fact or information back into your mind, you have not comprehended. Recall is your ability to remember what you have read. Top students usually put their text and notes on one side and try to recall the information they have read or studied.

**Review -** This is a formal assessment or examination of your reading endeavour with the possibility or intention of instituting a change. It is a critical appraisal of the text. If possible, read and re-read the text to check your understanding and clarify any points you were uncertain about.

**Why You Must Patronise a Library**

The truth is that a library plays a very important role in promoting your information gathering and knowledge acquisition. A wiseman said, "Knowledge is free at the library. Just bring your own container." When you understand the place and importance of library, you will not need someone to encourage you to patronise a library.

Top students know the value of library and how reading in the library could make a difference in their academic life. Apart from reading your recommended texts in the library you can also connect with ideas of great authors that you are not privileged to interact with one-on-one.

According to Norman Cousins, library is important because "A library is the delivery room for the birth of ideas, a place where history comes to life."

How can one prepare for any serious exams without researching for information and reading relevant books in the library? I can still vividly remember how I earnestly and devotedly patronised the state library while preparing for my JAMB exams in 1982. I am of firm conviction that library played a major role in my success story due to the fact that I had access to many books. Today, Young Disciples International, a youth ministry which I head, has established a community library at our youth centre for the reading public. We made it compulsory for participants of our training boot camps and Conferences to patronise the library.

# CHAPTER
## *6*
## Taking Hold Of Success Provoking Instructions

The honest truth is that instructions are healthy for your academic life and work. The Bible says, "Take fast hold of instruction; let her not go: keep her; for she is thy life." Prov 4:13

I have realised that excellent students are not more intelligent than other students. The difference is that they get ahead of others because they are more disciplined and focused, and have embraced academic-excellence-provoking instructions.

In this chapter, I'm presenting some instructions that will help you in the pursuit of your academic success, if you dare obey them.

1.      Don't wait until you're in the mood to read or study before you get down to work. Don't wait until you feel motivated before you start preparing for an exam.

2.      Develop the habit of writing important stuff down. This includes homework to be completed, test and exam dates, project deadlines, etc. Don't assume that you'll

be able to remember anything; write it all down to stay organised.

3.      Develop your own timetable! Write down your weekly schedule based on your academic commitments.

4.      Don't be distracted. Get rid of distractions before they become distractions. Don't be a back-bencher! Don't sit at the back of the class. Academic achievers minimize classroom distractions that interfere with learning. Restrict your Internet access. Don't allow your phone, TV, games, friends or anything to distract you!

5.      Make up your mind to be organised. Students who are not organised end up wasting precious time looking for items or notes, or doing last-minute work they forgot about. Set a daily reminder to check if there is any homework to do the following day. Set reminders to start preparing for tests and exams.

6.      Work towards breaking big tasks into smaller ones. Big tasks seem complicated and overwhelming, which is why some students procrastinate. Break every big task down into smaller tasks.

7.      Create a conducive studying environment. Ensure that the lighting in the room is suitable for academic work. Get a comfortable chair. Remove all distractions from the room.

8.      By all means try to take notes during class. It is foolhardy not to take notes in class. It is highly important to take notes in class, because it helps you to pay attention and to learn the concepts better.

9.      Don't forget to ask lots of questions! Asking your friends and teachers questions about what you are learning is a great way to stay engaged. It also ensures that you understand the new material. Don't be afraid of asking silly questions. Besides, if you pay attention in class, your questions will likely be logical and insightful.

10.     Take a few minutes to prepare for each class. A wise man once said, "By failing to prepare, you are preparing to fail." Preparing for class is something I encourage every student to do. Every night, think about the classes that you'll be having the following day in school. Take a few minutes to skim the textbook or notes, so that you'll be familiar with what your teacher will cover the next day. Do a quick recap of the previous topic, because the new topic will likely build on what you've already learned.

11.      Start studying for tests at least one to two weeks in advance. Cramming for tests is always a bad idea. I recommend that you set a reminder on your phone (or make a note in your planner) one to two weeks before every scheduled test, so that you'll start preparing for the test. For major exams, I recommend that you start studying four weeks in advance or more.

12.      Don't join the blame game! Don't blame anything or anybody for your academic woes. Do take full responsibility for your academic work. No blaming your teachers, parents or friends. No blaming the school principal or the government.

13.      Hang out with other students who are motivated and focused. You must be intentional about students you surround yourself with. Do you hang out with people who are pessimistic? Are they always complaining? Do they pursue excellence, or do they try to find shortcuts? Spend time with people who are in hot pursuit of academic success like you.

14.      Analyse the mistakes you made in tests and exams. It might not be a pleasant experience, but I encourage you to go through every mistake you made in tests and exams.

Analyse why you made such mistake. Ask yourself questions such as:

1. Was the mistake due to my carelessness?

2. Did I forget a key fact?

3. Did I have a poor understanding of a certain concept?

4. How can I make certain that I won't repeat the mistake?

5. What do I need to do to be better prepared for future tests?

This analysis will help you to make continual progress in your academics.


**Note of Warning!**

1. Don't get involved in any examination malpractice! If you are caught, you might be sent away from school. What a disgrace or an embarrassment to have your name published as a cheat. Don't allow shame or reproach be your portion or parents' lot.

# CHAPTER
## 7
## Knowing How To Engage The G- Factor

T he G-Factor is the God-factor in your academic
pursuit. It is the influence, and power of God
helping you in your academic work. Jesus Christ
says, "... for without me ye can do nothing." And this
includes your academic work. You cannot excel except
God is on your side. For you to excel in your studies, you
must learn how to depend on God for your success.
Without His help, you can do nothing! Except the Lord
builds your academic "house" you labor, study or read in
vain. The race is not to the swift! I urge you to depend on
God's grace for knowledge, wisdom and understanding in
all your subjects.

The Bible says, "As for these four children, God gave
them knowledge and skill in all learning and wisdom: and
Daniel had understanding in all visions and dreams."
(Daniel 1:17)

"And in all matters of wisdom and understanding, that the
king enquired of them, he found them ten times better
than all the magicians and astrologers that were in all his
realm." (Daniel 1:20) You need the God factor, if you
want to be highly knowledgeable and skilful in all learning.

You need the God-factor, if you want to be ten times better than all your classmates or course mates. It is the Lord that can make you have quick understanding! You just have to look up to Him!

The Bible says, "And the Lord will make you the head and not the tail; you shall be above only, and not beneath. . ." (Deut. 28:13)

God has promised to make you the head and not the tail academically, but you must agree with Him by accepting the personal responsibility to be successful. The Bible says, "Study to shew thyself approved unto God, a workman that needeth not to be ashamed, rightly dividing the word of truth."2 Timothy 2:15

You have the personal responsibility to read and study! Nobody can read or study for you!

Beloved, I usually feel so burdened when I see Christian students and even student-pastors fail in their examinations. The greatest joy of my heart is to see you excel and experience your God-ordained success. Academic success or failure is a choice. You can choose not to join the large percentage of those failing, and join the few that are excelling. The broad road of failure can contain large number of students who are not willing or prepared to take their academic work seriously. But I am of firm conviction that the narrow road of success can only and will only admit the determined, devoted, diligent, purpose-driven, and success-driven students.

As a way of provoking and motivating the G-factor, I would crave your indulgence to pray the following prayer points:

1.      Father God, in the name of Jesus Christ, I thank you for making me a student in the first place. Thank you for empowering my parents with financial resources to cater for my academic needs. Thank you also for giving me strength and health to face my academic work squarely.

2.      Father God, in the name of Jesus Christ, cause me to be highly interested in my academic work. Put in me the interest that will make me to get practically and actively involved in my studies.

3.      Father God, in the name of Jesus Christ, arise and bless me with the spirit of excellence in the order of Daniel and co! Oh God of Excellence, arise and cause me to excel in all my subjects so that I may bring glory to your name.

4.      Father God, I am determined to set and pursue my academic goals no matter the obstacle. Heavenly Father, kindly help me to follow through with all my goals with outstanding results in Jesus mighty name.

5.　　　Father God, in the name of Jesus Christ, I accept the responsibility for performance. I decide now to be a studious student. As I engage in a purposeful reading, help me to assimilate whatever I read.

6.　　　Father God, in the name of Jesus Christ, I commit into your hands my academic challenges. Help me not to be lazy and distracted. I come against every force of evil attacking my academic performance.

7.　　　Father God, give me the spirit of wisdom and understanding. Make me of quick understanding in all my subjects forthwith in Jesus name!

May I end this chapter with the outstanding success story of one of my sons in the Lord, Adeleye Adeyemi, a first class material from Obafemi Awolowo University, Ile-Ife, Nigeria! His success story gives credence to my postulation that God can use your academic success story to draw young men and women to Himself. I have his permission to use his testimony in this book, trusting God for the impartation of the grace that worked, and is still working in his life to work in your own life too, only if you can embrace his strategies.

Grace at Work "My academic success in school attracted people to me; my name went places I have never been-till date. Classmates wanted to find out what I was doing differently, junior colleagues wanted a guide. I had friends who were only close because they wanted to find out what was special about me but I was always happy to reveal to them that the special thing was God, God's grace. Grace was always the first and the last thing I mentioned whenever I was opportuned to counsel my classmates. Some 'battles' are not won in the examination hall; they are won in the secret place. My success has enabled me to preach the gospel in a way students want to listen. Many students are concerned only about their grades, and when they realize that this God you are talking about is the One who gives the power to succeed, they just but listen.

Academic success is a vital tool in student-evangelism! One of the many students that contacted me via my book just got converted to Christianity and she was facing a lot of persecution from her former religion. Knowing about me gave her much more courage and reasons to stick to her new faith and when we finally met in person I was more than sure she would be a vital tool in the hands of God.

I was a leader in both YDI and a campus fellowship. So the first conclusion people could make is that being committed to God does not remove from your capability to succeed; in fact I told everyone who cared to listen that God is the source of my academic exploit. One of my many resolutions at a time was as long as I remained a believer; no unbeliever would ever have a grade higher than me. To me, academic success is a way of showing forth God. It is a way of expressing His ability. He gave the Jewish boys an unusual aptitude in Babylon for only one reason: to show forth His glory and He still does the same thing today.

God's name was glorified as I graduated with the best result ever in my department in 2006 and as the best student also in my faculty. People who only knew me from afar as a Christian were left Wondering, "So something good still comes out of Nazareth..." While my success made more believers to hold fast to their faith, unbelievers were also attracted to the Promoter of men. I had classmates who wanted to be reading partners. I had those who wanted to be my friends. I had those who wanted to be in relationship with me. I had those who wanted to be mentored. I was not the best-dressed neither was I the 'most spiritual' person in the class but I had something everyone coveted: best results.

One of the most memorable counseling sessions I have ever had was with a classmate in my third year in the university, who still remains grateful till today. She was a believer and it was more than expedient for her to find a fellow believer who could encourage and instruct her in the way to go with the Word of God. It is always my deepest pleasure to share the scriptural principles of success with people and that was my greatest motivation for writing "The Academic god." Today, I mentor tons of

56

students and          success-oriented individuals both directly and via mails.

My outstanding success has put me in a privileged position that the younger folks look up to me and give me audience. What distinguishes me is that all I teach have scriptural foundations and I have lived what I teach with outstanding results to show forth. The light that shines on my candle of success has brought men to me whom I have also been able to show the source of the light: God. The Bible says, ". . .and let men see your good works that they may glorify your Father in heaven." My success also opens doors of service and capacity to influence.

During my tenure as the YDI president in Obafemi Awolowo University, lle-lfe, Nigeria, academic excellence was a priority because the members had a leader who was an example of academically successful Christians. Consciously and unconsciously, every member caught the vision of excellence and was better for it. Also, as a member of the YDi Hall of Faith, members of YDI were constantly, directly and indirectly prompted to aim at success because one of their leaders (and many others) has shown that spirituality is not a reason for mediocrity.

My success in school has also opened many doors of opportunity that may not have been if otherwise. My academic success qualified me for the E8 Education for

Sustainable Energy Development fellowship with which I am currently pursuing my Master's degree in USA, a great platform for shinning this little light of mine on and on. I have also had invitations to contribute to impact - making books and magazines and to speak in several nooks and crannies of Nigeria in churches, fellowships and schools as a reason of my results.

The world would have been worse off if only unbelievers are at the top of every area of our lives. In fact, every area of life where there is decadence today is usually crowded by those who don't know God. God has thus deposited in each of us an ability to work diligently, climb the ladder to the top and take over from the mean men so we can show men the way to Him.

Hence, God gives to everyman according to his ability and He expects each one of us to trade and make profit with what He gave. Day after day, I trade for the kingdom with my ability and I keep improving myself to ensure relevance. Academic excellence remains a vital tool in student-evangelism."

# APPENDIX

## Appendix A

### TALENT IS NEVER ENOUGH

On this fateful day, the lecturer for the free hand drawing course walked into the studio and gave her assignment. It was one of strangest things I've ever heard. She said with a soft laden but firm voice, "Please kindly pull one leg of your shoes, put it on the table and draw". Was she joking? The class first went into frenzy and then into a cold silence. When it was obvious our amiable lecturer was in for a serious work.

After a couple of hours, this drill was up for submission. And yes we all did submit. How I made it through, God knows but I did try my best. At another time, the assignment was, look through the window of our 3rd floor studio and draw the urbanscape and landscape you can see (buildings, roads, cars, trees, shrubs, streetlights e.t.c.). I'm sure this paints a picture of the scope of this task. Well, these and others were the kinds of assignments churned out weekly in the mandatory free hand drawing course in the school of architecture at covenant university where I obtained my architecture degrees.

Free hand drawing is one of the several courses I had to take as a pioneer architecture student at Covenant University. If I'm not mistaken, it is a 4 semester course across the first two years of the 4 year undergraduate architecture degree.

My academic journey may find some degree of analogy in the title of a book by John C. Maxwell: Talent Is Never Enough. Today, by the grace of God I'm a professionally registered architect. I graduated top of my class as the best graduating student for my Bachelor of Science and Master of Science degrees. I currently hold a PhD, and progressing further. I have over a decade of professional practice experience, with a portfolio spanning several building-types ranging from educational, health, recreational, residential, religious and institutional buildings.

I have also had the privilege of serving as the director, Physical Planning and Development, Covenant University. Looking back, I can only give thanks to God for His help. I recall with fond memories how Pastor Joe Ogbe, my pastor from my teenage years would refer to me as Prof. (short form for Professor). What he saw I can't fully understand, but I am grateful that I'm pacing into that future.

No one is born great. No one is born a genius. People grow into genius. Someone once said Genius is 1% inspiration and 99% perspiration. Studying architecture gave me a good sense of that statement. No doubt everyone is born with some natural talent and abilities i.e. tendency to do something with ease. A person may have talent in music while the other does not have but have talent with athletics.

The profession of Architecture is the art and science of designing buildings and some non-buildings. It is actually an artful science. This suggests that an architect needs to develop competence both in art and science. This development of dual competence is actually what makes architecture unique and yet a possible source of problem for many architecture students. Because, it does appear that humans generally have greater inclination either towards art or science.

In my case I happen to have greater inclination towards the sciences and I love architecture so I was qualified to study it. But in the first 2 years of the 4 year undergraduate segment of the 2 tier (4 years B.Sc and 2 years M.Sc.) architecture degree programme you are expected to have developed competence and an appreciation for the visual arts, particularly free hand drawing as part of the requisite skills to be a good designer. But obviously it didn't come as natural as I would have done in my architectural graphics/technical drawing (science based) and theory courses.

So the challenge for me and majority of architecture students was that architecture requires the development and engagement of both artistic and scientific skills set. Yet the student has greater inclination to either of the two, in my case I had greater inclination toward the scientific dimension than the artistic dimension. Also interestingly enough, while you engage the scientific (rational, analytic) skills in developing your design concepts, you communicate your design solutions and persuade your audience using the artistic dimension and consequently obtain thus good grades in school (patronage and clientele in business of architecture). So it appears I may have a 'rough' time in the school of architecture.

And so my journey began, attending classes and taking 10-12 courses per semester ranging from Mathematics, physics, general studies, computer appreciation, Free hand drawing (art based), Architectural graphics/ technical drawing (science and technical based) and others. At the end of my first semester after much effort and struggle, I had an E in free hand drawing and an A in Architectural graphics. So my inclinations were evident in my results.

By second semester with more effort and perhaps a more patient lecturer I had improved in visual communication with a C. And eventually at the end of 100 level, I had a CGPA (Cumulative Grade Point Average) of 4.34. A good result I must say and infact that was the best result in the

Architecture department. So I was gradually achieving my goals (though my goal was 4.50 and above).

A key learning point for me was that you could improve at anything you are strategically committed to. I was committed to my free hand drawing despite my limited natural ability in it and indeed I improved from an E to a C. While others spent 1 hour on a drawing task, I would put in about 2-3 hours to ensure I develop my free hand drawing skill. And oh! Yes, my free-hand drawing skills improved. As for my other theory courses I developed a strong reading schedule. Often times I would arrive at class by 6.30am for an 8.00am class to enable me secure a seat in front of the class and have ample time to read. Discipline was the watchword.

By 200 level, we entered into the mainstream of the Architecture program where you are expected to take lesser number of courses from the College of Science and Technology and more courses from the Department of Architecture. I had to take free hand drawing, architectural graphics, design studio and others. By this time the Design Studio was the priority course with the highest credit units of 4 units. The design studio in architecture requires you to solve human problems spatially and represent and communicate your solution visually. This visual communication of your solution is fundamental in any design discipline and that would require a combination of free hand drawing and architectural skills using the principles of architectural science and technology. So free hand drawing and design studio meant an increase in art.

Here am I with more strength in architectural graphics (science oriented) than free hand drawing (art oriented), and yet Design studio requires a combination of the two skills and free hand as course on its own is art based. So the strength to forge ahead was less than half. My chances of success about 50:50. But I was determined to succeed. Nothing will do, but success.

So I had to re-strategize by spending more time in the free hand drawing and the design studio. My result was far from desired. I made a B in Design Studio, and a C or B in free hand drawing and dropped in my other courses compared to my 100 level. My CGPA dropped from 4.34 to 3.87 by the end of the 2nd year. Wow, I goofed. I was devastated.

In my drive to ensure success in free hand drawing and design studio, I spent so much time more than necessary on them at the detriment of my other theory courses. In a bid to perform well in design studio and free hand drawing, I totally neglected my other theory courses with over confidence that I had a retentive memory. I barely read any note or textbook during the entire session. Rather, I was consumed in Design studio. And really this wasn't specific to only me. It was a class syndrome.

Because this was the first time we were taking design studio; the defining and differentiating course in the school of architecture. Studio was time consuming, mentally demanding and physically draining. In fact, the typical architecture student sleeps in the studio to keep up with submission schedules. A couple of my classmates would even skip classes to have sufficient time to meet up with studio submissions. I wasn't left out. I missed a couple of classes and missed some assignments in my theory courses.

Design studio was consuming. Failure in design studio meant an extra year. In fact, a memorable experience I had in my first Design Studio assignment was on anthropometrics (the science of measuring the size and proportions of the human body especially as applied to the design of furniture and machines). The anthropometrics assignment was really a grueling one with limited submission time. I had to stay awake for 54 hours at a stretch (2 days and 6 hours) at a stretch towards the completion of the assignment. My desire to succeed in the Design Studio put me on overdrive that I forgot and neglected my other courses and the result was devastating at least to me because of the high goals I had set for myself.

Well, the learning point from my 200 level experiences is, balance. You must learn to balance your many aspirations. Like a general at the war front there are no small enemies. Every enemy is dangerous and can destroy you. So, give appropriate attention to every enemy. In like manner, balance is the key. Give every course you are studying the required attention needed. You must learn to juggle several balls together.

As I moved into my third year, penultimate year to completing my B.Sc in Architecture, I got more matured. I was the more resolute to turn the tides in my academics. I have now learnt the need for my balance in my several multi-varied courses, design still demanded more of my time. But I have learnt how to give or allocate my time better among my different courses. Obviously my grades improved and my CGPA got better.

By the time I was concluding my year 4, I graduated with a CGPA of around 4.24, making me the best graduating student. Though I didn't make a 1st class, I had given my very best. And interesting enough I had an overall performance beyond my colleagues, some who were seemingly more talented than I was in the artistic dimension, which influenced their design. But I had worked my way and used my scientific and engineering competencies to impact my design. Thus, what I lacked in one area I made up for it in the other.

Getting in for my masters of science degree in architecture was apparently a lesser challenge because I had gained a mastery of my areas of deficiencies and evolved my unique style. At the time I was concluding my M.Sc programme, I finished with a 4.81 CGPA. This is a distinction grade and I emerged as the best graduating student again. Wow! My dreams came through, a first class result and the best graduating student.

**Dr. G. M. Alalade, (Ydi Fellow)**
Covenant University, Ota

# Appendix B

I have realised over the years that success in life and everything we do can be traced to three major pillars:

1.    Arduous work

2.    Consistency

3.    The favour of God

Outside these three pillars, success will only be a mirage.

While getting ready for college, I remember having a conversation with someone who had graduated from college and he talked about how college was different from high school and the difficulty in attaining certain levels of academic excellence such as a first class. My response to him was "They told me the same thing when I was about entering high school, but guess what, high school was not as difficult as they painted it." He perhaps felt I was too naïve to understand his point, but I was not going to let fear get into me. I went to college with the mentality that it was not going to be as difficult as they made it seem and by God's grace, I graduated summa cum laude from college.

**Learning Point:** The mindset with which you approach a project will largely influence the outcome of that project. Peoples' experiences of a process does not automatically define yours. It is good to take advice from people, but do not let them instil fear in you through their advice. Getting into college, I saw various kinds of people with diverse backgrounds. Some went to the best of schools while some others attended average high schools. Some had multiple A's in their WAEC result while some others were just average. Personally, I knew I did not attend the best of high schools in town, but I was determined not to allow myself to be intimidated by my colleagues' background or achievements. I made sure I put in enough effort to reading and understanding my courses. The outcome of this was that I ended in the top 6% of my class.

**Learning Point:** Everyday, life gives us a new opportunity to direct the course of our lives. It is a new page, clean slate, tabular rasar, for us to start again, hence we should not allow the past successes of others make us feel we are incapable of achieving so much. As a freshman, the starting line is the same for everybody.

As part of my resolve to be the best I could at college, I decided I was going to attend all lectures, write my notes myself and make sure I study consistently. I knew I had to attend all lectures because I realised that it was easier for me to understand a subject when I listen to the lecturer teach it and I interpret my understanding in my notes myself during the class. So, while studying later, I would easily picture the lecturer and what he/she said at each point in time.

**Lesson Point:** Discover yourself and figure out the learning style that works for you. We were all created differently with unique gifts and learning styles. Some people may not attend a single lecture, but once they are able to study the lecture notes, they understand perfectly. For some people, they understand a course after reading it once, while some others would have to read a course more than once. Remember, it is an individual race.

The other thing I decided to do was to ensure that I had complete understanding of whatever topic the lecturer was teaching. To do this, whenever I had difficulty understanding a concept, I would often refer to different textbooks in the library that explained the same concept. In some other instances, I would look for videos on youtube that explain the concept I am trying to grasp. By getting different perspectives from multiple sources regarding a topic, I realise that I have a better understanding of that subject matter.

**Lesson Point:** There are times you will have to go the extra mile to understand something or achieve a certain objective. The lecturer's perspective may not be sufficient for your understanding, or it may be that the lecturer is unable to communicate a point in a way that would make you understand. Once the lecturer has taught a topic, the onus is on you to understand it by any means possible.

I recall in my first year in college, I was led to organise a tutorial for my course mates on one of the courses we were taking. I realised that some of my colleagues were having difficulties understanding some parts of the course while I had a better understanding. During the tutorial, I noticed one or two strange faces, but I did not mind, I went ahead to teach and answer questions. To my surprise, I realised one of the strange faces was a carry-over student, and she thanked me for organising the tutorial. After this, I heard the Spirit of God say to me, "I did not make you intelligent for yourself alone, but for the people around you". Ever since then, I made it a point of duty to always organise tutorials for difficult courses every semester. One amazing thing I learnt during the process was that, I had to go the extra mile to make sure I understand a topic well enough to not just pass an exam, but to be able to teach people.

The implication of this was that I had a better understanding of the difficult courses, hence it was easy for me to pass the exams.

**Lesson Point:** Compassion is a critical success factor. In the process of helping people get better, you are indirectly helping yourself get better. There are some perspectives regarding a subject that you may never get unless you try explaining to someone and the person asks you a question on it. Hoarding knowledge is a sign of mediocrity.

God taught me a lesson in my second year. I recall in the first semester of my second year in college, I attended lectures and wrote my notes as usual, and I decided to study more than ever for my exams. To do this, I would leave my hostel for the library or classroom and pretty much spend the entire day there. I did this consistently for a while and I was so sure I was going to have fantastic grades at the end of that semester. To my greatest surprise, I had my lowest result ever in that semester. I was confused and dejected. I knew I had put in so much effort into that exam and was expecting more. I tried talking to lecturers of some courses I thought I should have gotten a better grade in, but they did not hear me out. So, I decided to let go and move on.

A few weeks into my second semester after I had seen my first semester result, the Spirit of the Lord made me realise that the reason I had the result I did was that I depended too much on my efforts. I went into the exam hall with confidence in the fact that I have studied well for the course. And as such, I left no room for God to perform His wonders.

With this revelation, during my second semester exam, I studied adequately, but at the same time, I recognised my inadequacy and asked God to take control at every point in time. I had my second highest result in college in that semester.

**Lesson Point:** Trust in the Lord with all your heart and lean not on your own understanding; in all your ways submit to him, and he will make your paths straight - Proverbs 3:5-6. Many times, we are so much confident in our abilities that we fail to recognise that God plays a role in the outcome of every endeavour. Hard work and commitment will not produce much if done without the favour of God.

At some point in college, I started wearing different leadership hats; in my service unit in church, my departmental association, and the college of development studies and more were still coming. This started telling on me as my attention was now being shared amongst several things and I had limited time to focus on the main reason for my being in college; academics. In order not to lose focus on my academics, I had to cut down on my extracurricular activities and limit my involvement to two activities; my service unit and my department. With this, I remained relevant to my church community and my department also.

**Lesson Point:** It is important to engage in extracurricular activities in college, but this should not be at the detriment of one's academics. Remember, the main reason you were sent to college is for you to get a degree. If you win every award there is to be won in college without a college degree, you would not graduate. Hence, it is important to keep your eyes on the ball.

Sometime in my third year, I was gloomy because I noticed that whenever I organised tutorials, people attend, understand what is being taught, sit for the exam and they have A's while I end up having B's in some of the courses. While trying to snap out of that mood, the Holy Spirit left a scripture in my heart; "and let us not be weary in well doing: for in due season we shall reap, if we faint not"- Galatians 6:9. This scripture encouraged me and gave me strength to continue organising the tutorials.

Fast forward to few weeks post NYSC when I was trying to get a job, my coursemate back in college sent me a message asking if I had gotten a job. I told her I was yet to get a job and she asked me to send my CV…to cut the long story short, by God's grace, I got a job at the company she was working for. This former coursemate of mine used to attend the tutorials then.

**Lesson Point:** "And let us not be weary in well doing: for in due season we shall reap, if we faint not"- Galatians 6:9. God works in mysterious ways and His thoughts are way ahead of your thoughts. Whenever He asks you to do something or to continue in a process when you feel like giving up, listen and do what He says. It may not look like it now, but trust me, God has everything planned out.

In your pursuit for academic excellence, everything you need to be outstanding is within you. Nobody came to this world with any knowledge of mathematics, economics, engineering or whatever. Every outstanding person in various fields came to this world the same way as you did. The difference between them and every other person are the steps they took, the level of work they put in, their consistency and the favour of God.

Remember, you have the mind of Christ, hence you can comprehend all things no matter how difficult.

Warm regards,
**Segun Afolabi, (Ydi Fellow)**
First Class, Economics
Covenant University, Ota.

# Appendix C

## ACADEMIC EXCELLENCE FOR YOUTHS

Daniel 2 v 9 "…I Daniel, understood by books…"

My academic excellence journey has inspired a lot of people and even myself. With a mum that's a teacher, it was quite expected that I was going to be smart.

I started school also early and the results have always been good. I remember playing a lot in primary school but still seeing good results. I got all distinctions in my Junior secondary school exams even though I got a double promotion from JSS1 to 3 which is a rare occurrence in the secondary school system in Nigeria. But things got a little skewed as I got into the senior secondary classes. I had opted to get into the Art class contrary to everyone's advice to stay in the sciences and become an engineer or doctor. Stubbornness or purpose, I really cannot tell. I just knew I wanted to be different and make a mark with my difference.

By this time, I had gone through YDLI, (a YDI leadership training programme) and just had a passion for being the different one in class.

I didn't do so well in my SSCE, in fact I had an F9 in Christian Religious Studies. Maybe proof of how bad my standing with God at the time had become. With such stain, my admission to law in UNILAG was delayed and denied. Then, I went on to study Computer operations. Still waiting for admission, I went on to study French and civil law before I got admission into Babcock University in 2010.

I got into school as a YD. I had attended 4 Camp Joseph meetings by this time and I had witnessed young people in University doing exploits. In fact, 2008 thereabout, the Academic god as he is fondly called had graduated top of his class with a First Class at Obafemi Awolowo University (OAU) and had always won the awards for excellence at Camp. I knew I wanted such and I prayed for it before I resumed.

The formula was simple. Get to school, read your books well, go to every class, research well for your assignments, add extra touches every time, walk closely with God and just excel. But there was a secret the Academic god shared at one of our meetings: write 100 points on every of your note books and strive to make 100, not 70 or 80. I obeyed and did same. I would start every semester aiming to hit 100. I understood how to calculate my cumulative grade point average; I found out what the grading system was like at Babcock and asked my seniors how to make A's in the courses I was offering.

It was as simple as the above system but as rigorous as passing a thread through a needle's eye at night. Possible but with hard work and dedication.

My semesters were great. I was on a first class from my first semester till I finished. My least GPA was a 4.69 and I graduated with a 4.81 to God's glory. But it only got better when I first heard from God in 2011 of how I was going to make a 5.0 GP three times during alone with God at Camp Joseph. And so the following principles helped me make such good results at University and even afterwards at the Nigerian law school.

1.        **Hearing from God.** Faith (belief, total trust in God and His awesome power and spirit) comes by hearing and hearing the word of God. When you walk closely with God there is a rub off of excellence on you by the things you hear. Once saved, you can hear Him because He deposits the Holy spirit inside you. I remember I always prayed that the Holy spirit should teach me things I didn't understand, and He always did.

First thing I ask people when they complain about grades is: what does God say about your academics? Do you know exactly what He wants you to come out with? You might not have a word that says He wants me to have a 4.7 CGPA or to be the best in Mathematics this year. No. But you may be inspired by your network to be the best at something and know always that the Holy spirit in you cannot be at work and you would be on the lower percentile of the class. Get the word of God concerning your identity and walk in victory.

2.      **Deliberate Variety Study:** Being a high-flying student means that you are vast and deep in various subjects. Spend time not only reading about your choice course of study but also on self-development, related topics, current affairs, history, economics and your faith. You become wiser, deeper and more knowledgeable with these subjects and can give a wider view to answers especially in more theoretical courses.

3.      **Set Goals:** This is as important as waking up. You must see a finish line and have a strategy on getting there. The goal is to come out the best you can come out. Systems are created to allow for possibilities. Therefore, you must break free from any mentality that limits you to thinking you cannot make good grades. A and F grades exist because people can get them. So set the goal to hit the best mark and work towards it. Read, study, discuss the subjects, relate them to practical things and keep them in memory that way. Also have a goal tracker and be accountable to yourself in constant reviews to know what you did badly at and how you can get better at something on your strategy.

4.      **Research:** Find out from friends and senior colleagues how to hit the mark you want to hit. It is important to note that you cannot learn how to build a duplex from someone who built a mud hut. You can however ask the man who aimed at building a duplex and ended up building a mud hut to know what he failed at and learn from the experience. You must ask questions

and find out the how, the why and what to do to make good grades at any course or even life endeavor.

5. **Values:** What values do you stand for and how do those values translate into workable life principles that can aid your work at school? Curiosity, adventure, creativity, communication, integrity, honesty, are some values that you should search yourself to know. Knowing yourself is critical in this journey. It helps you know what can work and what cannot work for you. If you are creative and would rather get better ideas when you go on trips to nature sites, find such and go there to study. Most schools have botanical gardens where your creativity can be unlocked. When you know yourself it's easier to move through challenges that may come with studying and you pace yourself correctly. In all, you must strive to know and acquire character in knowledge.

6. **Reward System:** I used to reward myself for every A I got in my mid-semester exams and the semester itself. As from a very interesting background, Shawarma gave me great joy when I made good grades. For some other people, their parents help by buying them cars and other toys when they get good grades. Reward yourself by yourself. You earned it, you worked for it, and you got it. It will make you more responsible to yourself than others. It might not be buying something for yourself, it might just be taking yourself out.

7.     **Help Others:** There is power in raising others. There is no great deal in a one-eyed man in the land of blind men if he cannot actually teach the blind men some efficiencies. You must learn to never look down on your friends and younger colleagues who need some extra help with studying or even understanding concepts that you believe are simple because you have grace to simplify them. Someone said that we often teach others the things we need to know best. In teaching others, we become masters in the literal and figurative sense of it.

You must STUDY hard and read your books! There is no two ways to it. Whether you are smart or have natural abilities, you must read those books to know what is in them. We have understanding easier because we have the mind of Christ, the Holy spirit in our inside that teaches us and reminds us of things. So nothing to worry about. Having the right network that you walk with is great, as that will help solidify these things. For me, YDI is a great place to have that right network. And outside YDI, I have great friends and contemporaries that inspire and challenge me to be a better version of myself.

Remember, do not to be in competition with anyone but yourself. Be the best you can be. Just set the goal, read your books, ask for understanding, follow a strategy, and be great at what you do! God bless you!

**Okezi Meshack, (Ydi Fellow)**
First Class, Law

Babcock University

If you are struggling academically, do consult me for counseling and prayers.

joejesimiel2006@yahoo.com

Facebook- Joe Jesimiel Ogbe

# Other Books By The Author

1.     Teenagers and Relationships

2.     The Youth God Uses

3.     Building an Effective youth ministry

4.     Can Boys and Girls also go to Hell?

5.     Securing your Marital Destiny

6.     Questions that Singles Ask

7.     How to Obtain Favour from God and Man

8.     Pathways to a Blissful Courtship

9.     Becoming Rich and Wealthy

10.     Strategies for a stress-free Relationship

11.     Enjoying God's Mercy

12.     Getting what you want by Faith

13.     Hebrew Women's Style (Divine Tips for mothers to be

14.     Praying for Divine Blessings

15.     Youth and Friendship

16.     Youth and Opportunity

www.ingramcontent.com/pod-product-compliance
Lightning Source LLC
Chambersburg PA
CBHW071907020426
42331CB00010B/2705